* * * * *

'This empowering book creates a world where being yourself is fully celebrated. With practical and creative activities, *Trans Survival Workbook* holds your hand as you make space to unapologetically explore and express who you are. An important reminder to all that gender has no recipe!'

– Gendered Intelligence

'This is an engaging and powerful book, relatable and friendly whilst unpicking some of the stereotypes and encouraging young people to express themselves freely and document their own personal journey in a way that celebrates their individuality and uniqueness. I loved it and would thoroughly recommend it alongside the excellent *Trans Teen Survival Guide.*'

– Susie Green, CEO of Mermaids

'With wisdom, compassion and just the right amount of slapstick comedy, Owl and Fox Fisher take the fear and stress out of questioning gender. They are our family and best friends, guiding us along our trans, non-binary and gender non-conforming journeys.'

– Kate Bornstein, Gender Outlaw

'Whether you are transgender or cisgender, an ally or activist, a parent or child, this is the book for you. A workbook full of evocative words and illustrations, where you choose YOUR colours to help you on your gender identity journey or understand someone else's with kindness, consideration and care.'

– Tash Walker, Co-Chair of Switchboard LGBT+ Helpline

* * * * *

First published in Great Britain in 2021 by Jessica Kingsley Publishers
An Hachette Company

1

Copyright © Owl and Fox Fisher 2021
Illustrations copyright © Fox Fisher 2021
Illustrations on pp.63–65 copyright © Nicoz Balboa Zanchi 2021
Illustrations on pp.93–94 copyright © Rory Midhani 2021
Illustrations on pp.98–99 copyright © Sophie Labelle 2021
Illustrations on pp.112–113 copyright © Lewis Hancox 2021

Age Disclaimer: Please be advised that some of the advice and guidance
in this book is only suitable for people aged 18+.

Trigger Warning: This book mentions dysphoria.

A CIP catalogue record for this title is available from the British Library
and the Library of Congress

ISBN 978 1 78775 629 8
eISBN 978 1 78775 630 4

Printed and bound in Great Britain by Bell & Bain Limited

Jessica Kingsley Publishers' policy is to use papers that are natural,
renewable and recyclable products and made from wood grown
in sustainable forests. The logging and manufacturing processes
are expected to conform to the environmental regulations
of the country of origin.

Jessica Kingsley Publishers
Carmelite House
50 Victoria Embankment
London EC4Y 0DZ

www.jkp.com

TRANS Survival Workbook

Owl and fox FISHER

Jessica Kingsley Publishers
London and Philadelphia

Dear Friend,

We've tried our hardest to be compassionate and sensitive when creating this book, and to try to make sure everyone feels safe and supported by it. But we are also aware that we all have such different experiences and ways of seeing life. So if you feel something isn't quite right, feel free to skip some parts or come back to them later. This workbook is about you, so do whatever makes you feel good.

The *Trans Survival Workbook* is a personal journal that takes you on a creative journey designed to help you reflect on who you are, and what your gender and expression mean to you.

Welcome

...to your own personal *Trans Survival Workbook*!

Regardless of your age, we think this journal will definitely be of use to you!

In this book we will explore what it means to be you in more creative terms than we did in our previous book, the *Trans Teen Survival Guide*.

While that book was packed with information, we also wanted to offer you a chance to reflect more personally on your gender identity.

In this book we will be using transgender as an inclusive umbrella term for everyone who does not identify with the gender they were assigned at birth, including non-binary people.

The accompanying PDFs can be downloaded from https://library.jkp.com/redeem using the code UFAEXVZ

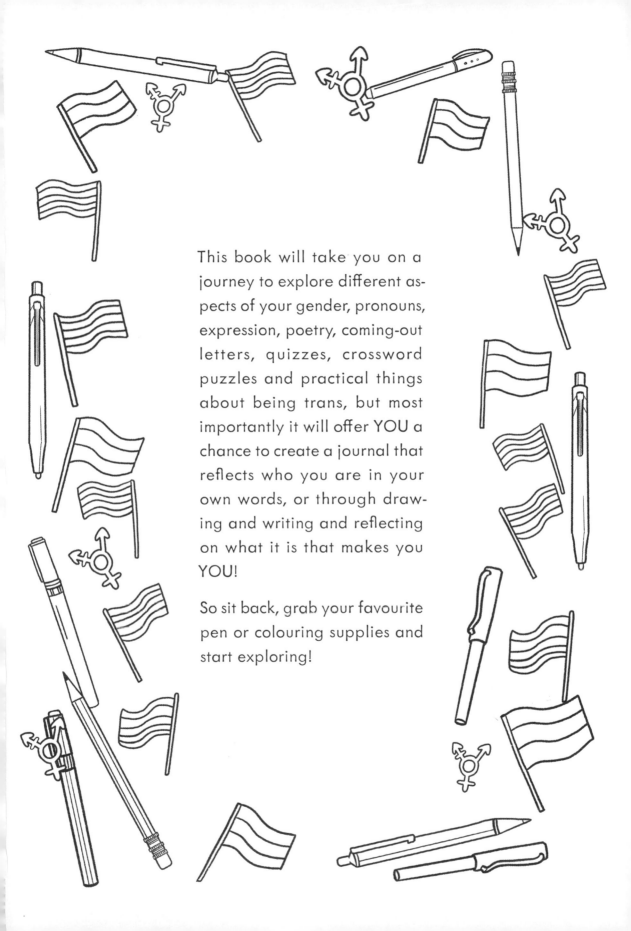

This book will take you on a journey to explore different aspects of your gender, pronouns, expression, poetry, coming-out letters, quizzes, crossword puzzles and practical things about being trans, but most importantly it will offer YOU a chance to create a journal that reflects who you are in your own words, or through drawing and writing and reflecting on what it is that makes you YOU!

So sit back, grab your favourite pen or colouring supplies and start exploring!

It's a...

Everyone's obsessed with gender. From the moment we are born, and now often even way before, people obsess over whether someone's going to be born a girl or a boy. They plan ahead of time, prepare nursery rooms in certain colours and even hold gender reveal parties where everyone is invited to celebrate the genitalia of their new baby. That then becomes a symbol of who we are going to be: a boy or a girl.

But this doesn't always work — which is something that trans people (and intersex people) are all too aware of. While almost everything about us is expected to evolve, change and take new forms, our gender is something that people see as destiny, or something that can never change. But we all know that everything changes at some point. When it comes to gender, it seems that society has accepted certain changes but not others, and those of us who stray too far from the mould are seen as 'different'.

It's a bit like cake. Okay, hear us out on this. We all agree that a certain combination of ingredients will most certainly create a lemon drizzle – the rind and lemon drops that give it a tangy taste, the soft and moist centre is made with the right combination of dry and wet baking ingredients, and it's drizzled with sugary yet sour goodness on top. Mhh! No two cakes are the same, really – but we still accept that they are all cakes if they fulfill certain criteria. Once the cake starts becoming something different, for example if it takes a different shape, we change the ingredients, the flavour...is suddenly becomes something different.

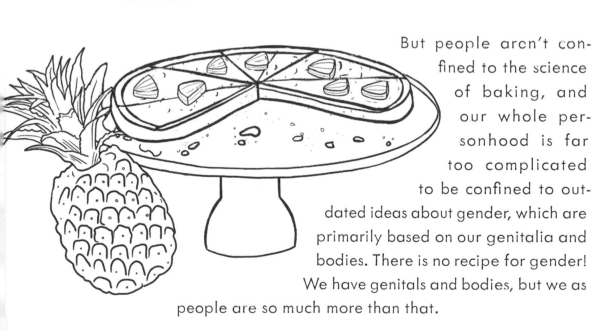

But people aren't confined to the science of baking, and our whole personhood is far too complicated to be confined to outdated ideas about gender, which are primarily based on our genitalia and bodies. There is no recipe for gender! We have genitals and bodies, but we as people are so much more than that.

But this book isn't about theory, or justifying why we exist and how the world is much more beautifully diverse. We know it is. This workbook is about you, and is meant to be an affirming space where you don't have to justify yourself to anyone.

This is a space for you to be yourself in the most authentic way possible, so savour it and forget about all that other stuff. Let's start with thinking about who you are, and what that means to you.

This workbook might not always be easy – and there might be times when you need to take a break, think about things, laugh, scream or even cry. So don't be too hard on yourself, and never feel like you have to apologize. Remember to be kind to yourself and that you're the only one in charge of who you are. No one or nothing else can define you, and your gender identity – whether that's being a non-binary person, being a woman, being a man – is entirely and completely valid. Your expression, body or other people's perception of you don't define you. It's your life, so you get to decide how you want to live it.

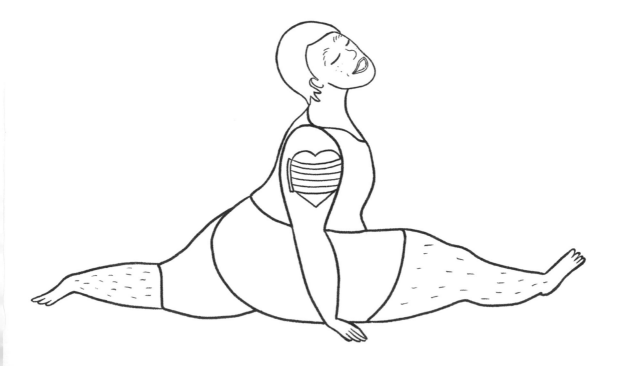

Hello

MY NAME IS:

MY PRONOUNS ARE:

THEY/THEM

HE/HIM

SHE/HER

PLEASE USE MY
NAME INSTEAD
OF PRONOUNS

OTHER:

PRONOUNS ARE
FOR INFERIOR
BEINGS, MORTAL

MY GENDER IDENTITY
I AM

(pick as many as you want):

a trans woman

a trans man

non-binary

trans masculine

trans feminine

genderfluid

genderqueer

agender

pangender

bigender

demigirl

demiboy

a cisgender woman

a cisgender man

Not listed? Write it here:

There are many ways of describing our identities, but often we get bogged down into quite academic or complicated language.

If you were to describe who you are using more creative ways, such as in a song or spoken word piece or even describing it via colours, landscape or a specific feeling, how would you describe your gender identity?

A purple flower in a field of yellow flowers, that all sway in the wind on a warm summer's day? A raindrop in a green pond? That feeling of complete bliss when you crawl into bed after a long day?

Feel free to let your imagination run wild, either with words, colours or pictures!

A CREATIVE
EXPRESSION OF
MY GENDER

Expression is how we show who we are outwardly, e.g. via clothing, make up, hair, style and demeanour.

Traditionally women present themselves as feminine and men as masculine, and most people assume that non-binary people are all androgynous/masculine.

But thankfully society is a lot more diverse than that, and within all genders, people have so many different ways of expressing themselves. The most important thing in all of this is to express yourself in a way that makes you comfortable. There is no right or wrong way to express yourself, so even if you're a tomboy or a femme boy or a non-binary person who isn't androgynous, you're just as valid. Your expression does not govern who you are as a person.

Have a think about what your expression is now, whether you're comfortable with that or whether you'd like to express yourself differently. What is your ideal way to express yourself via visual means?

MY GENDER EXPRESSION

How would you describe your gender expression?

....

....

....

What makes you feel more like yourself when you get dressed?

....

....

....

What type of style do you prefer?

....

....

....

Do you use make up? If so, what sort of make up?

....

....

....

What fictional character's style do you most relate to?

....

....

....

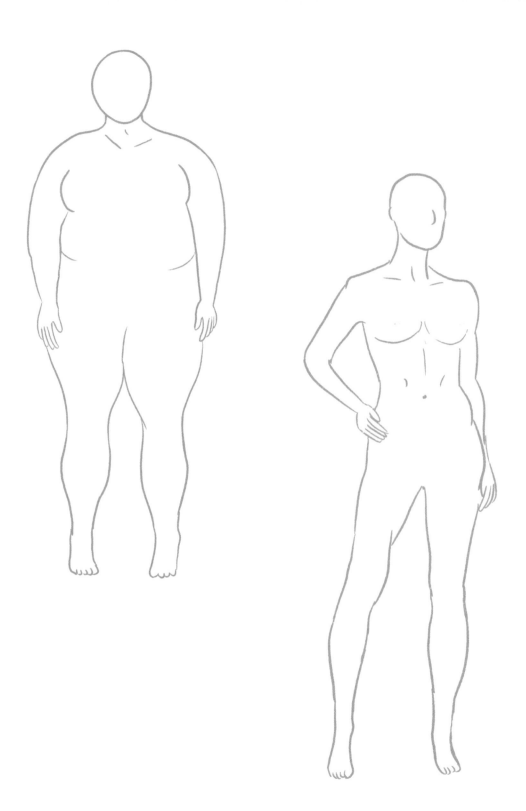

CREATE SOME GENDER EXPRESSIONS FOR THESE PEOPLE

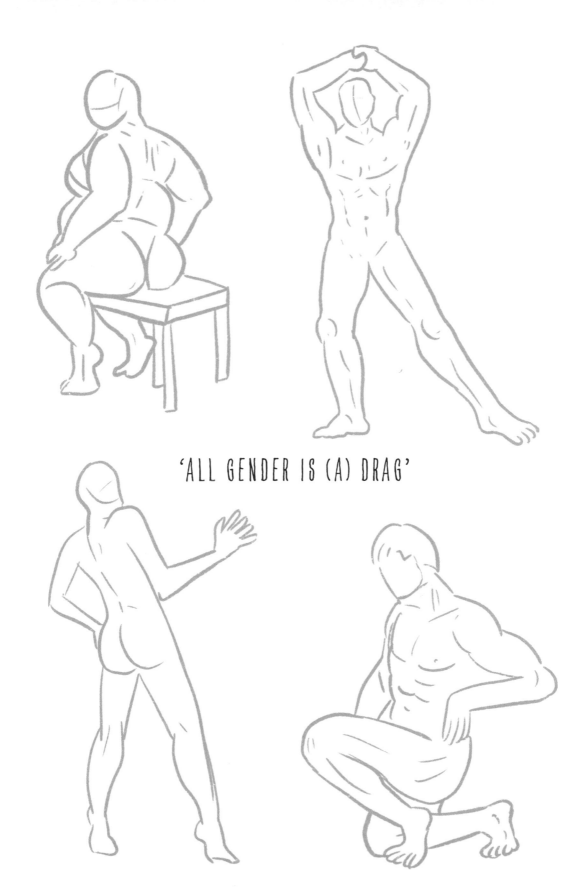

'ALL GENDER IS (A) DRAG'

MY PRONOUNS ARE:

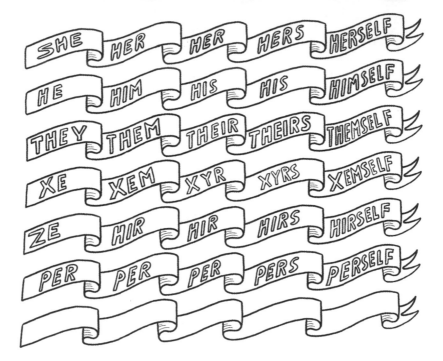

SHE · HER · HER · HERS · HERSELF

HE · HIM · HIS · HIS · HIMSELF

THEY · THEM · THEIR · THEIRS · THEMSELF

XE · XEM · XYR · XYRS · XEMSELF

ZE · HIR · HIR · HIRS · HIRSELF

PER · PER · PER · PERS · PERSELF

HEY! RESPECT MY PRONOUNS PLEASE

Pronouns are really important to us. Anyone who's changed their pronouns to reflect who they really are will definitely know the euphoria when someone uses the correct one.

That's why it's so important to also respect everyone else's pronoun, even if we haven't heard it or don't get it. The most common ones are obviously he, she or they pronouns, but different communities or countries might have their own set of pronouns.

What do your pronouns mean to you, and what does it feel like when people use the correct one? What about when people use the wrong one?

Write a short story involving two people. Give one character gender-neutral pronouns. The story must also involve a hat, a rabbit or both.

Taking a closer look at who you are

There are many things that affect who we are and how we are seen by others. Different factors will have an effect on how we are treated by others and how we navigate spaces in society. Here are a few factors that usually contribute to a degree to who we are in this big wide world:

Gender	Sexual orientation	Looks	Weight
Race	Mental health	Neurodiversity	Language(s)
Ability	Political beliefs	Citizenship	Family
Class	Habitat	Residency	Money
Age	Religion	Sex characteristics	Job

Are your differences something you always notice? Do some give you an advantage? A disadvantage? Have a think about all of these factors and whether they affect your life, and whether they do so negatively, positively or have no effect.

Putting Yourself First = Winning at Life

What can you do today, perhaps even right now, that will help you feel more comfortable?

This can be literally anything you can think of, and shouldn't warrant any type of stress, guilt or overbearing commitment.

Try doing this at least once or twice a day for a week, and write down if anything has changed for you or it has helped you somehow.

THE RATHER DIFFICULT
TRANS-THEMED WORD SEARCH

The words can be horizontal, vertical or diagonal.
How many words can you find?

Hint: they're officially all trans-related words (and a few secret extras)

```
V Y F D Y S P H O R I A A U G W Q A J S H Z P M
R L U Z T W Q V A S Q H D C W U X H M Y S Y H B
B X T T L U E Y B I G E N D E R S M Z I Z K A T
B E O D O R C M A R U D Q H N W J I P D A G L S
C V N O V T Q M F S J Y U B Q E B I V E F K L P
B A P E E T R A N S G G N D E R L D K N Z B O A
B L I D G N O N B I N A R Y V B O U E T E K P N
G I G E E Y G C X W L N F P T H C H U I X I L G
E D X M N A C J N Q P M K U G B K V S T P B A E
N I G I D U J S G W O V Z B X I E T U Y R E S N
D E X B E D E M I G I R L E B N R U E L E U T D
E V O O R Y G E N D E R V R E D S C X X S P Y E
R X V Y Q U B B R J Q G A T M E M K X E S H R R
F P Z X U R C H B D K A F Y O R P I E E I O P F
L S T O E X W W E E I Y D U G Z Z N T U O R U T
U A B R E H F E T A Y R E O U K B G W A N I D R
I F A U R Z F B V A G I N O P L A S T Y C A E A
D H A P P I N E S S E W N W Y X N J T Q D Z H N
L E I N D C T E S T O S T E R O N E R Z F H K S
P U K M U X O E S T R O G E N A G E N D E R A W
W U V Y R N G Q J O Y D F C X P X U R E A L D O
U A C P D E A D N A M E N X X E L H K H S K S M
H T P A C K E R I L J U M A S T E C T O M Y L A
Y O A N L V N V Z T R A N S M A N J K O S W I N
```

Struggling? Flip forward to the next pages for all the 26 trans-themed
words in the puzzle and simple definitions of each word.

Terminology

The most important thing to remember about terminology is that there isn't one way to define something. Terms are constantly changing and evolving and can differ between countries and contexts, so getting too hung up on the 'correct' way to define something can often be counter-productive or a waste of our time. There are many ways to say the same thing, and it's okay if we don't all use the exact same words.

Terms can offer us such a valuable insight into who we are, but not everyone has access to the same type of language or opportunities to discuss them in depth. Some people grew up in a different time and find solace in words we might deem outdated nowadays. Terminology is something we use to describe ourselves, and we should be wary of telling others what they can or cannot call themselves.

But we also have to be careful not to appropriate terms from other cultures that have huge cultural significance, such as hijra in the Indian community, two-spirit in the Native American community or kathoey in Southeast Asian communities.

Here are a few short explanations of the terms in the word search, which in no way are the exclusive definitions of these trans-related words. They are just suggestions based on our own perceptions and understanding of these terms. Your definition might be different or you might even disagree – that's fine! This is YOUR workbook, so you can do or think whatever you want here.

SHORT AND SNAPPY DEFINITIONS

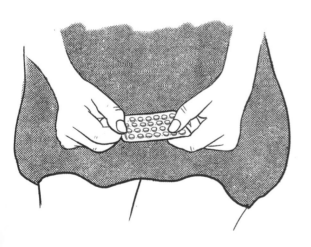

Agender: Someone who feels the absence of gender.

Bigender: Someone whose gender is both a man and a woman at the same time.

Binders: A top/vest used to flatten someone's chest and alleviate dysphoria.

Blockers: Medication used to pause the effects of puberty.

Deadname: A trans person's old name, which they do not use anymore.

Demiboy: Someone who identifies partially, not but fully, as a boy.

Demigirl: Someone who identifies partially, but not fully, as a girl.

Dysphoria: Distress that occurs when your physical characteristics and/or people's perceptions of you don't fit with your inner sense of self.

Gender: A social construct that defines what is a boy, a girl or a non-binary person. Sometimes used interchangeably with gender identity.

(Gender) expression: How you express your gender outwardly, i.e. through clothing and style.

(Gender) identity: Your inner sense of self in terms of gender.

Genderfluid: Someone who experiences their gender as fluid, e.g. feeling that your gender goes between feeling more feminine, to more masculine, and anything in between.

Genderqueer: Someone who doesn't identify with conventional categories of gender.

Mastectomy: A type of top surgery.

Non-binary: A term used to describe people who aren't exclusively men or women, e.g. people who are fluid, in between, both or completely outside of the gender binary.

Oestrogen: A hormone that feminizes the body.

Packer: A detachable penis and balls.

Pangender: Someone who feels they encompass all genders at once.

Phalloplasty: Genital surgery where a penis is made.

Puberty: A stage in your physical development when hormones start to drastically change your sex characteristics.

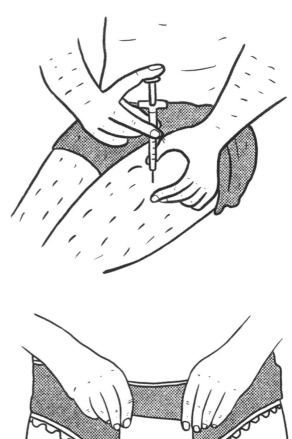

Testosterone: A hormone that masculinizes the body.

Trans man: A man who was assigned female at birth.

Trans woman: A woman who was assigned male at birth.

Trans(gender): An umbrella term for all people who don't identify with the gender they were assigned at birth.

Tucking: An act that is used to hide a bulge from showing through clothing.

Vaginoplasty: Genital surgery where a vagina is made.

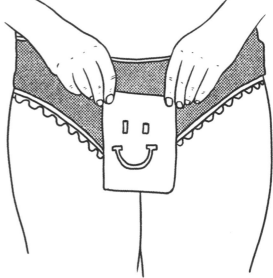

Create some trans-positive tattoos:

COMING OUT

Coming out as trans can be scary. But life is too short to hide away who you are out of fear of how others might react.

It's important that you stay true to yourself and live your life for you, and not anyone else. Taking that step is often the hardest part, and once you've done it you will feel so much better about yourself. It might not instantly feel good, especially if people respond negatively. But ultimately, you'll know that it was the right thing to do. Above all, make sure you are safe and that you have some place to go.

There are various ways to do it, whether that's speaking to people in person, sending them a message or writing them a letter.

In this next section we'd like to invite you to write your own coming-out letter. Think of who you'd like to address it to and how you'd like to explain it. If you've already done this, either re-write your coming-out letter/announcement, or print it out and fit it into the next section.

YOUR COMING-OUT LETTER

Useful things to consider include:

- Who are you sending it to?

- Explain briefly and in simple terms what it is to be trans

- Explain who you really are, and what your identity is now

- Are you going to be using a new name from now on?

- Are you going to want them to start using different pronouns?

- Mention what changes you'll be going through in the next few years

- What you'd like to happen from now on

- A few words of reassurance that you're still you, but you'll become a happier version now that they will know the real you

- Offer them resources or places to find more information and support if needed

- Invite them to talk to you about it further

MY COMING-OUT SONG

Coming out can be really nerve-wracking, especially when you're unsure if people around you are going to understand. How would you describe coming out in more creative terms? If you were to create a song or rap, what would the lyrics be like? If you've already made something like that, plop it in!

Steps to making a song:

1. Start with a beat (instrumental)

2. Come up with a hook (chorus)

3. Write lyrics for a verse

Extra credit:

4. Practise and record

5. Make a music video

Things that help me to feel good about myself

BE ~~WITH~~ SOMEONE WHO MAKES YOU HAPPY

NOT A PHASE

AND SO WHAT IF IT IS?

Chances are that you've identified as one or more letters of the LGBTQIA+ umbrella at some point in your life, or you currently inhabit more than one! We, the creators, certainly have, and at one point or another in our lives we've pretty much been all of them!

Have a think about what it's like to have that journey from one identity to another and why people might explore themselves in this way. Is it because that's simply who they are and how they've matured, or is it because they have been searching for the right term and finally realized who they really were?

How did it make you feel when you had another identity? Did it fit? Did you enjoy it? Do you miss it?

If you didn't come out as anything else first, what did it feel like to find a definition that fit?

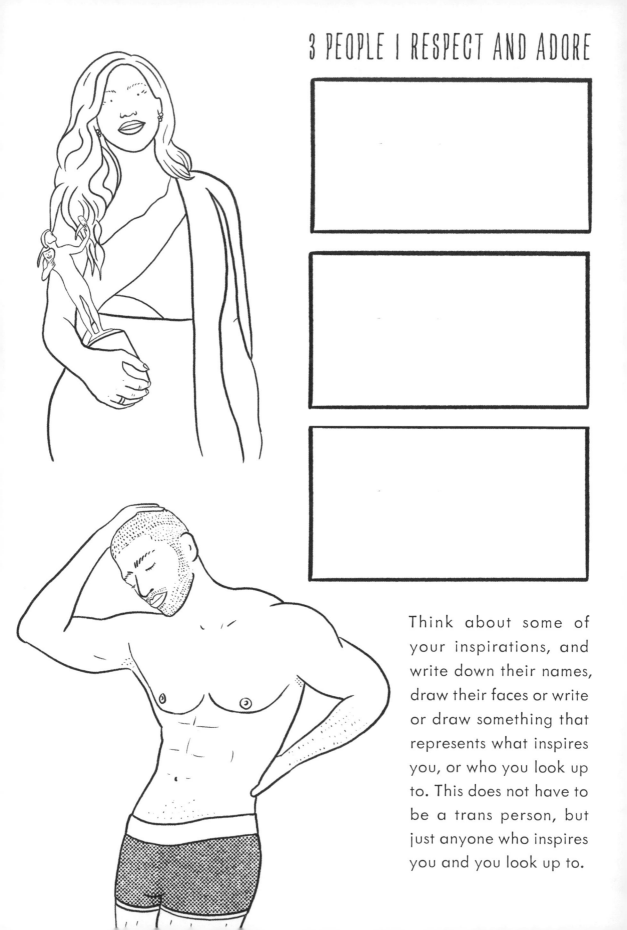

Think about some of your inspirations, and write down their names, draw their faces or write or draw something that represents what inspires you, or who you look up to. This does not have to be a trans person, but just anyone who inspires you and you look up to.

We have many inspirations, and one of them is undoubtedly Kate Bornstein and their *My New Gender Workbook*. In their book, they had a wonderful light-hearted and non-serious quiz that helped you figure out your gender, and we thought we would do something similar with you too. So welcome to the ultimate quiz of finding out your gender! It is not an actual gender quiz though, so do not fret. But it can be fun!

It is quite simple – just tick what box feels most appropriate to each question, round up the numbers and calculate your result! A bit like an online quiz, except instead of the computer doing it all for you, you have to do it yourself. Old school, we know.

THE
ULTIMATE
GENDER
QUIZ
(not really though)
KATE BORNSTEIN STYLE

THE ULTIMATE GENDER QUIZ (NOT REALLY THOUGH) KATE BORNSTEIN STYLE

Part 1: Reflection

1. Which of the following statements is the closest to describing who you are in terms of gender?

a) A girl/woman or a boy/man

b) Mostly a girl/woman or a boy/man

c) Non-binary

d) If none of the above fits, please specify:

_____

e) I'm gender everything (or nothing!)

2. What pronouns do you use?

a) She/her or he/his

b) She/her or he/his and they/them

c) They/them pronouns

d) If none of the above, please specify:

_____

e) Just use my name

Part 2: Expression

3. What best describes your gender expression?

a) Feminine

b) Masculine

c) Androgynous

d) Who cares?

e) Chaos

4. Would you say that your gender expression matches what people expect based on your gender identity, i.e. are you a girl/woman who has a feminine expression?

a) Yes, my expression is quite conventional

b) My gender expression doesn't match people's expectations of me

c) My gender expression varies a lot

d) My gender expression cannot be contained

e) Gender expression? Who needs that?

5. Do you shave your body hair?

a) Yes, I really dislike body hair

b) No, having body hair is like the best thing ever!

c) Well, sometimes. Depends on how I'm feeling, really

d) Sometimes I grow my facial hair and match it with something more stereotypically feminine

e) I'm a furball

6. Have you had 'the op'?

a) Yes! It's the best

b) No, I don't want surgery

c) I've had trans-related surgery/surgeries, if that's what you mean

d) Don't ever ask anyone that question ever again

e) I don't know what that means

7. Do you ever feel limited by people's perceptions of you?

a) No, people usually just see me as me

b) I definitely don't go into details about my gender unless they are trans themselves, or really good allies

c) Yes! I wish people were able to see beyond their binary perceptions of gender and bodies

d) No, because I don't care what other people think of me

e) This isn't even my final form!

8. When someone refers to you as a 'beautiful woman', what is your reaction?

a) Total bliss

b) Could be worse

c) Utter despair

d) Muttering quietly to yourself: Beauty is a social construct

e) Start humming the 'Oh, Pretty Woman' themesong

9. Has someone ever told you that you're not real enough?

a) No

b) Yes

c) Yes, and I have sometimes felt like that myself

d) Most people actually don't believe my gender identity is valid

e) I'm a dragon, what do you think?

10. Do you think your gender expression might change at some point?

a) No, not really. I think I've found my comfort spot

b) It might, but not drastically

c) It's always in a constant state of flux

d) I think it might change quite dramatically at some point

e) It's The Neverending Gender-Bending Story!

Part 3: Your place in the world

11. Do people usually use your correct pronouns unprompted?

a) Yes, always

b) No, but most of the time

c) Hardly, I always have to correct people

d) I use gender-neutral pronouns, and regularly get into a conversation about how a singular 'they' has existed in the English language since the Shakespearean era

e) I don't care for pronouns

12. Has anyone ever questioned your gender?

a) No, not really

b) Sometimes people do, but most of the time people assume correctly

c) People constantly question who I am, and regularly misgender me

d) My gender confuses the hell out of people, and I want to keep it that way

e) I'm not sure I understand the question?

Part 4: Desires and romantic and sexual orientation

13. How comfortable are you with having sex?

a) I feel/felt uncomfortable having sex without having undergone genital surgery

b) I'm really comfortable with having sex and I am quite active

c) I am comfortable with having sex with the right people

d) I don't like having sex at all

e) I've never had sex

14. Do you have a type?

a) Yes, I always fall for the same type of people

b) Usually, although usually the same gender

c) I'm quite fluid in terms of gender, but there are certain characteristics and expression I'm attracted to

d) The emotional connection matters to me more than gender or expression

e) I don't really fall for people at all

15. Have you had a one-night stand?

a) No, but would like to

b) No, and couldn't think of anything worse!

c) Yes, and it was really awkward!

d) Yes, many times and it's great. 10/10 would do again

e) I've already told you that I don't like to have sex! Give an ace a break here

16. Are you usually the...

a) Top

b) Bottom (power or otherwise)

c) Versatile – out of all the flavours, why be salty?

d) I don't prescribe to limiting sexual behaviour terms

e) I. DON'T. LIKE. SEX. OKAY?

Part 5: Limitations and flexibility

17. How many genders really exist?

a) Only two, right?

b) About 72 according to Facebook?

c) Depends on who you ask. I think there are more than we realize

d) You mean you haven't heard of us non-binary people? We're real, and coming for your gender!

e) Foolish humans, confining themselves to pointless binary social constructs

18. Do you ever play with your gender expression?

a) No, I like to keep to a certain expression only

b) Rarely, but maybe if a good occasion came up I would

c) Yes, I try different things out all the time

d) If playing with gender expression was an Olympic sport, I'd be a gold medallist

e) No, but gender expression likes to play with me

19. If you can't tell someone's gender, how does that make you feel?

a) Uncomfortable. I need to know!

b) Very curious

c) A bit intrigued, but it's not really my business anyway

d) Solidarity!

e) That feeling of the breeze against my furry face when I'm flying high up in the sky... Wait, what was the question?

Part 6: Your expectations

20. Did you think this was going to be a serious quiz?

a) Wait, what?

b) Yes! I was really looking forward to finally getting accurate results about my gender!

c) Well, I thought it might be kinda fun

d) I can't believe I've lasted up until this point. Obviously no quiz was ever going to determine my gender

e) I don't know what the hell is going on here!

Rounding it up:

Okay, time to round up your score! The scoring system is really quite simple.

For all a) options: 1 point

For all b) options: 2 points

For all c) options: 3 points

For all d) options: 4 points

For all e) options: 5 points

Part 1 score: _____

Part 2 score: _____

Part 3 score: _____

Part 4 score: _____

Part 5 score: _____

Part 6 score: _____

Total score: _____

20–30 points: The Good Old Classic

Sometimes the classics are always the best. In your case, you like to keep it quite simple, meaning that you're most likely just a typical girl or a guy trying to make their place in the world. You might think that makes you somehow boring, but it doesn't. You're still a badass trans person who's surviving despite all the odds, and just because your gender might be classic or even basic, it doesn't mean that you're not breaking the mould in other areas of your life. You're more than just trans, you know?

31–50: The Gender Explorer

If you want to be my lover, you gotta, you gotta support the trans community! While you might mostly be quite conventional in your gender and expression, there are parts of you that just want to be something else, or you're just not that hung up about gender anyway. It doesn't make you uncomfortable to try different things, because you know who you are. You've got more important things to do than worry about gender, right?

51–70: The Gender Bender

Your gender identity, sexuality and gender expression doesn't really fall neatly into any conventional categories. You're something more than that, nothing at all or simply something completely different. You probably constantly have to explain to people who you really are, and you really fuck with people's ideas about gender. In a world with so many possibilities, why be binary?

71–90: Destroyer of Gender

You know what? Screw gender. You see gender as an oppressive construct that must be deconstructed and completely reformed. Nothing good has ever come from gender, so why are we keeping it, right? You don't really care for those rules and you're constantly breaking them – but it also means you know exactly how to use them to your advantage. Maybe one day we'll have a society where gender doesn't govern what we do or who we are in society, and that's a future you're fighting for.

91+: Falkor, the Luck Dragon

Falkor, why are you taking this quiz? You're a fictional luck dragon! We know gender means absolutely nothing to you, so why are you here as opposed to in *The Neverending Story*? What is this, The Neverending Gender-Bending Story? Geez, these luck dragons.

DYSPHORIA
AND HOW TO MANAGE IT...

Anyone who experiences dysphoria knows that is can be incredibly difficult. Dysphoria can be crippling and keep us from being active and doing what we want to do out of fear or distress about how we look or how people perceive us. It's important to be kind to yourself and try to find ways to cope with the dysphoria, whether that's by doing something nice for yourself, talking about it with a friend or a therapist or whatever helps you.

That's why we've assembled a list of things you could do to make yourself feel better, in hopes that it will help you alleviate some of your dysphoria or at least offer you some things to do to distract your mind and calm you down.

Be kind to yourself

Allow yourself to enjoy and pamper yourself. Walk a dog, make your favourite meal and binge watch your favourite show. Light a nice candle or incense (eco-friendly of course) and surround yourself with good and supportive friends, or hang out by yourself and read a good book or play a video game.

Experiment with clothing and expression

You could get a haircut, or try a different type of jacket that either hides or highlights certain parts of your body. Clothing can really help us shape and achieve a certain look, so think about what type of clothing helps you achieve the look you're going for. Baggy hoodies might be ideal to help you alleviate your chest dysphoria, and packing could help you feel better about lower dysphoria. Things like tucking, binding and using breast padding can also help, depending on what fits you and your expression.

Get creative

Write a song. Create art. Write a poem. Write a screenplay. There are so many ways in which we can channel our dysphoria and transness into art, or completely forget ourselves and create something different to divert our mind. Ever taken a screen-printing course? You could be the next Andy Warhol.

Remind yourself things are going to be okay

We all have times when we feel down or overwhelmed, but it's important not to lose sight of the bigger picture. Remind yourself that you're on a journey. Take a look at your transition chart (that is further along in the book) and see where you're at now, where you've been and what your goals are. It's all going to be okay.

Surround yourself with friends and people who accept you

It's important to seek out environments that are supportive and where you don't feel judged. This could be a support group in your local area, an online forum, videos by a trans person or a good therapist. If you're able, getting therapy is a really great way to help you out, not just with being trans, but life in general. Getting help is not something to be ashamed of, but something everyone should aspire to do.

Tend to your hobbies

Read a book, watch a TV show, play a video game. Garden. Cook. Get on a roller derby team. Anything that you enjoy doing will inevitably help you feel better, or at least distract your mind.

Practice mindfulness

Mediate, do some yoga. Do breathing exercises. Even physical exercise if that's your fancy. Many people find real solace in tending to their body and mind in various ways.

Tidy around the house

Some people get a real kick out of cleaning their house and tidying around them. It can be good to evaluate all your belongings and be mindful of what you own and whether you need all of this stuff. Donating to charity and finally clearing out that cupboard you've stuffed can be a good way to distract yourself.

Build a pillow fort

Sometimes it's just that kind of day. Build a pillow fort and hide yourself inside it with a laptop or a phone or a good book. Pillow forts are the best.

WHAT MY DYSPHORIA LOOKS LIKE

WHAT MY GENDER EUPHORIA LOOKS LIKE

What advice would you give to someone to alleviate dysphoria? Are there any particular things you do?

Reminder

Not all trans people experience dysphoria, and the level of dysphoria people feel differs depending on where people are in their journey. Dysphoria can also manifest in many ways, and can be social, physical or a mix of both. All trans experiences are valid, and we should never tell someone they can't be trans just because they have different experiences from us.

Let's remember to be kind and compassionate towards each other and not put those who are different to us down. We've got enough going on, so let's show solidarity with all our siblings and be the change we want to see in society.

Even though there might be things you don't like about your body, there are bound to be things you do like, like your hair, your hands, your legs, your lips or your eyes. Maybe you even adore everything about your body! Write a love letter to your body, declaring all the things you appreciate and love about yourself. If you're not in that space yet, that's okay too. You can come back to this once you are there, or even write about where you are now and where you want to be.

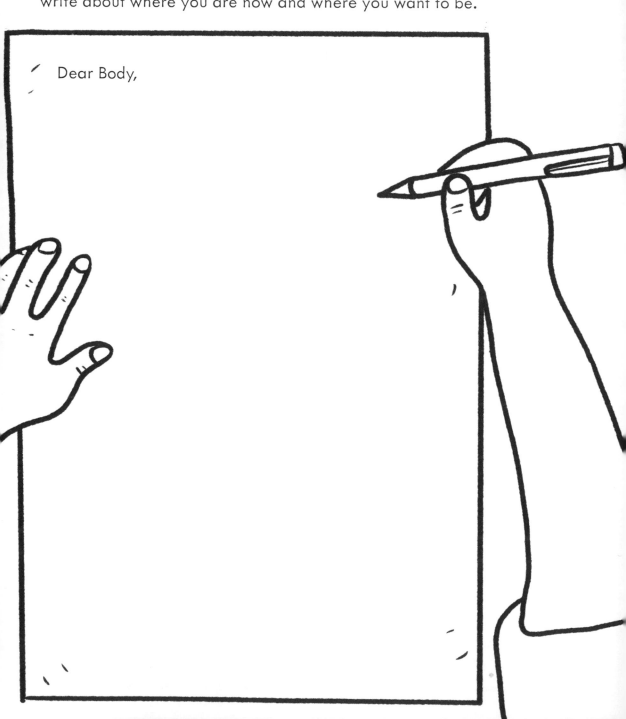

Dear Body,

Time to unlearn some of that internalized transphobia! We're relentlessly bombarded with negative content and media about trans people, with all the hardships and how awful it is to be trans. But what are some of the good things about being trans? The friends you've made? The community you belong to? A unique life experience? All the great hair colours and styles? The great memes? Have a think about the things you like about being trans and the things you appreciate.

What I like about being trans

AWKWARD TRANS TALES

'I often forget people don't know I'm a trans man. Last week I was telling a story and started with, "When I was a waitress"...cue very confused looks and me hurriedly switching it to waiter!'

'I took a tumble at roller derby and my breastforms fell out. Cue a desperate scrabble to recover them and get them back in place unobtrusively which is a bit hard when you've just hit the floor with a bang.'

'One time I wore a packer at the gym and it flipped out of place while I was on a bicycle and I had to run to the bathroom covering my crotch to get rid of the giant bulge in my pants.'

'My co-worker saw old pictures of me with my shirt off, flexing, and holding a rifle and he refused to believe it was me. I had to point out a hand tattoo before he accepted it was a pic of me and not my husband. My co-worker didn't know I was trans for six months. #validating'

'During my top surgery pre-op appointment, they found a lump and I was sent to get it scanned. I still had boobs at this point, and the nurses that did the scan thought I was cis and had gynecomastia. They asked me how long I'd had it and why. They felt really sorry for me.'

'I'm registered male on my GP records. Met a new GP, said I had a burning pee hole and he asked to see my dick. I coyly replied I didn't have one and that he probably should have checked my notes before I entered the room. Pretty certain it has trans male written all over my file.'

'I was stood at a bus stop with two neighbours. One knew me as my deadname, the other didn't. So when the first neighbour referred to me with my deadname, I sheepishly had to explain that was no longer my name. I wanted the ground to swallow me up.'

AWKWARD AND SORT OF FUNNY...?

We've all been there. As trans people, our lives are often riddled with awkwardness and painful and funny moments (maybe not at the time, but in hindsight!). Write down or make a comic strip about an awkward trans tale.

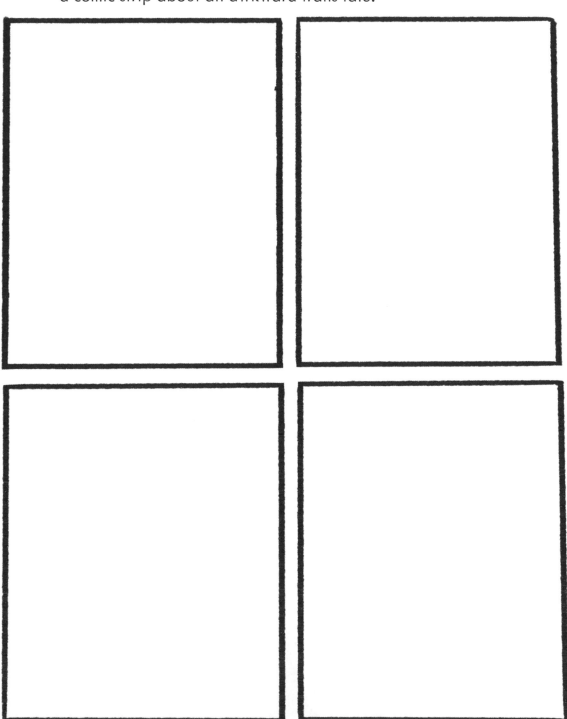

DOCUMENTING MY JOURNEY

Sometimes our inside doesn't quite match the outside. As trans people, many of us are painfully aware of this. But what is your ideal self? Take a moment to reflect on this. Draw a picture of your ideal self (which could very well be a picture of your current self, mind you!) or find a picture of someone that you'd like to look like and stick it in here (or find whatever visual representation you want that best fits who you are).

**A picture of someone that inspires
what you'd like to look like**

DESIGN SOME PATCHES FOR YOUR FRIEND'S JACKET

CHARTING MY TRANSITION

Sometimes creating a vision board of your goals or where you want to go is helpful.

Have a think about where you are in your transition (whether that be social, medical or a mix of both) and chart out the goals you have reached or want to reach.

Then station yourself somewhere along that chart to get a feeling for where you are and what you want to achieve.

Try thinking of it as an empowerment exercise and set yourself goals to create a better future for yourself.

This might feel a bit overwhelming, especially if you are at the start of your transition, but it's also helpful to set goals and know exactly where you're going.

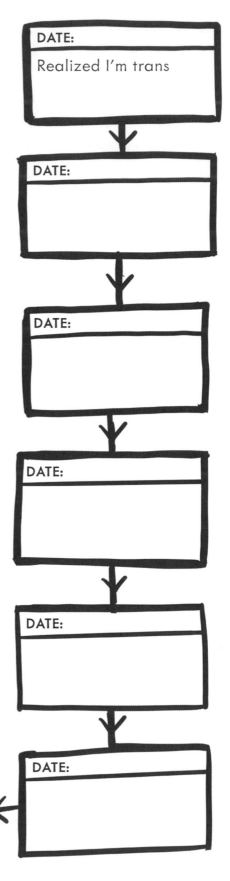

DATE:

Realized I'm trans

DATE:

DATE:

DATE:

DATE:

DATE:

DATE:

DATE:

Trans bingo! If any of these applies to you, or it's something that's ever been said to you, cross it out!

Anti-cistamines	Have you had the op?	But what's your real name?	I never would have guessed!	Dyed hair
Haircuts are terrifying	Shock at pre-transition photos	How do you have sex?	People harassing you are also attracted to you	Random Twitter user lecturing you about trans issues
Trans trenders	Trans genderism/Trans gendered	TERF FREE ZONE	VOICE	Video games
They/them pronouns are plural only	Which bathroom do you use?	But RuPaul said it!	Dead naming	Euphoria when gendered correctly
The cis are at it again	cHrOMo soMeS	So can you get pregnant?	Terrified of phone calls	BODY HAIR

The most important thing when you're on a journey to become yourself is to remember that you are unique and no one else can be like you. So while you might have aspirations to be like someone you saw or someone who's been on this journey for quite some time, it's important not to put yourself down. You have to remember that whoever you are is also beautiful, valid and totally amazing!

You never know where your journey might take you, and it's all about finding that comfort place and loving yourself. It's a never-ending journey (or a never-ending story like our friend Falkor might say), so we shouldn't constantly be waiting to love ourselves until we've reached a certain step. Sure, it will be awesome and make us feel great once we achieve certain things, but we also have to remember to be kind to ourselves along the way.

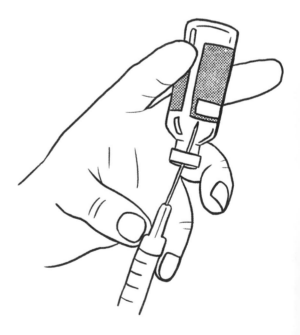

WISH LIST

List all the things you want to achieve in order to be your ideal self and how to get there. This doesn't have to be just physical things – think about who you are as a person and what achievements or steps you can make to be your ideal self. This includes aspirations for the future: set yourself some goals, decide what you want to spend your time doing, if you want a partner, a family, a campervan, a cat, or whatever it is that you feel contributes to you being your ideal self. Once you're written your list, take a few moments to imagine how you will feel once you have everything.

A binder is an item of clothing used to press down breasts in order to alleviate chest dysphoria. The most important thing to remember when binding is to BE SAFE. If you're not doing it right or if you're doing it for too long at a time, it can be severely dangerous to your physical health. Here are a few things to keep in mind.

- Only wear binders that are approved and tested to work.

- Never use tape, bandages or any unapproved method to bind.

- Make sure you're buying the right size binder, as a binder that's too small can be dangerous to wear.

- If you start to feel pain in your ribs or chest, your binder is probably too small and/or you've worn it for too long. Take it off as soon as possible.

- Regularly consult your healthcare specialist and have check-ups to prevent yourself from causing long-term damage by wearing a binder.

- Take regular breaks throughout the day.

- Never wear your binder for more than eight hours max at a time.

- Never sleep in your binder.

TOP TIP: FOR LONGEVITY AND COMFORT, TRY WEARING A T-SHIRT OR VEST UNDER YOUR BINDER

MY BINDER

Binder type:	
Brand:	
Size:	
Year bought:	
Average use per day (hours):	
Any problems?	

MONITORING USAGE

In order to make sure you're not binding for too long at a time, try monitoring how long you're wearing it each day by filling in this table for a week. If you're wearing it for more than eight hours a day, you'll have to start thinking of how you can cut down binding times to prevent you from causing damage to your body.

MON	TUES	WED	THURS	FRI	SAT	SUN

TUCKING

Tucking is when someone tucks their penis and testicles in order to not have a bulge visible through their clothes. This can help alleviate dysphoria. There are a few ways to tuck, but the most common way is with tape or gaff (or a combination of both). Gaff is a type of fabric (often in the form of underwear) that tightly holds things in place when worn. Some people like to tuck their testicles as well, although not everybody does. On the next page we have a few tips on how to tuck safely.

TUCKING SAFELY

1) Tucking the testes

In order to tuck your testes, you gently push them up and inwards into the natural canal on either side of your pelvis. Voila! They should have naturally vanished into the canal.

This might feel uncomfortable for the first few times you do it, so make sure you test this carefully and stop again if it's uncomfortable. Try it a few times in your own time before committing to it fully.

Your testes naturally slip back out if you move your legs wide enough apart and shimmy them back down, so don't worry about them getting stuck there! In case you're scared to do it, you can also gently tuck them back along with the penis and secure with tight gaff pants.

2) Tucking the penis

This involves taking the penis and gently tucking it between your bum cheeks. It can either be held in place with sports tape or medical tape, or with a gaff.

When using tape: If you're using tape, you can wrap a piece of tissue around the penis (to protect the skin) and then wrap the tape around that and tuck it behind and secure the tape at the back.

When using gaff: Simply tuck the penis (and the balls, if needed) between your bum cheeks and slip the pants on to hold it in place. Both tape and gaff can be used as a combination, too.

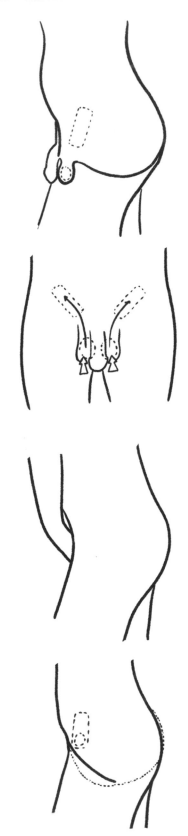

To keep in mind:

- If it hurts, stop. Take a break. Try again, but more gently. Tucking might feel slightly uncomfortable for the first few times, but it should never hurt.
- Don't do it for too long. Untuck when you can, or try wearing clothing that doesn't require tucking.
- Take good care of your skin and the area, and make sure you're not irritating the skin, getting sore or unclean.
- You can't pee while tucked! Every time you need to pee you'll have to untuck. But don't put off peeing just because you're tucked. That increases the likelihood of you contracting a urinary tract infection, so never sacrifice your physical needs for the sake of tucking. Be responsible and safe at all times. If it starts to hurt, you need to untuck and take a break.

MONITORING USAGE

In order to make sure you're not tucking for too long at a time, try monitoring how long you're wearing it each day by filling in this table for a week. If you're tucking for more than a few hours at a time, you'll have to start thinking of how you can cut down tucking times to protect the area and not damage it.

MON	TUES	WED	THURS	FRI	SAT	SUN

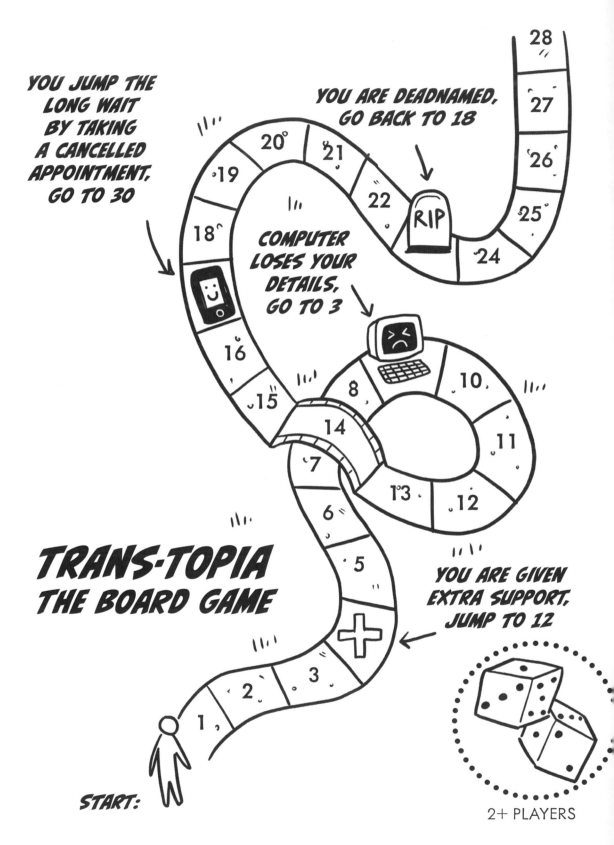

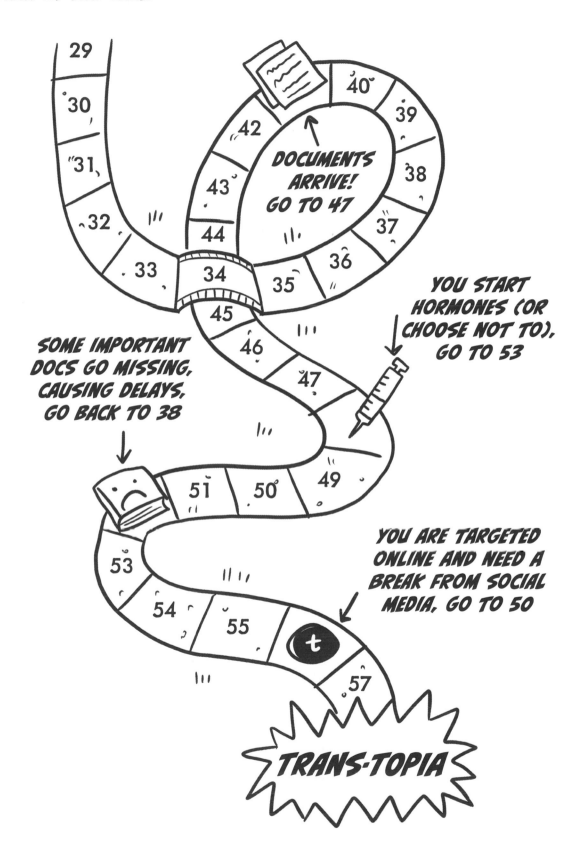

BACK IN THE GAME

DOCUMENTS ARRIVE! GO TO 47

YOU START HORMONES (OR CHOOSE NOT TO), GO TO 53

SOME IMPORTANT DOCS GO MISSING, CAUSING DELAYS, GO BACK TO 38

YOU ARE TARGETED ONLINE AND NEED A BREAK FROM SOCIAL MEDIA, GO TO 50

TRANS-TOPIA

On screen, what trans people or shows have inspired you?

Create a fictional series with a trans theme/character.
Write a short synopsis of the show here:

Draw a scene from the show:

If you're non-binary (or someone who is asked to explain the term to others), you'll know that it's often difficult to explain to people what it means. How would you explain non-binary issues to someone with zero understanding of this identity? If you're not sure, now's the time to do your research! Write your thoughts below.

Create some wording for the placards

Add your own trans-positive statement

Which fits you the best? Tag urself!

Venus
- = capitalism must end
- = home-made cheese
- = yoga
- = eats cis people

Hiccup
- = always says the wrong thing
- = wasn't listening
- = cannot stay still
- = forgets they are trans

Pickles
- = goth AF
- = possibly a vampire
- = trans patches and badges galore
- = finger guns

Fluffers
- = a bit of a mess
- = shy & bi & trans
- = who needs furniture when you can have plants
- = anime

Crème Brûlée
- = trans memes for days
- = uses video games to be themselves
- = doesn't leave house for days at a time
- = OwO

Velvet
- = angrily corrects people
- = just angry
- = really needs cuddles
- = aaaAAAAAaaaaa

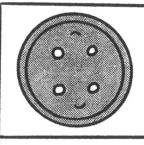

Button
- = responsible
- = knows all the queer definitions by heart
- = cries when angry
- = will fight you

Plant-Based Nugget
- = the mom friend™
- = /r/trans
- = herbs
- = finishes your food

LONG WAITING TIMES GOT ME LIKE

MAKE YOUR OWN MEME

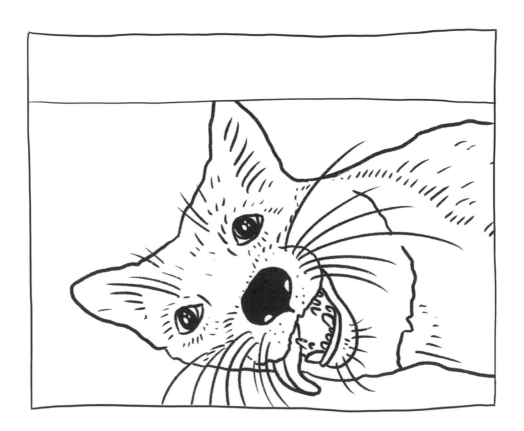

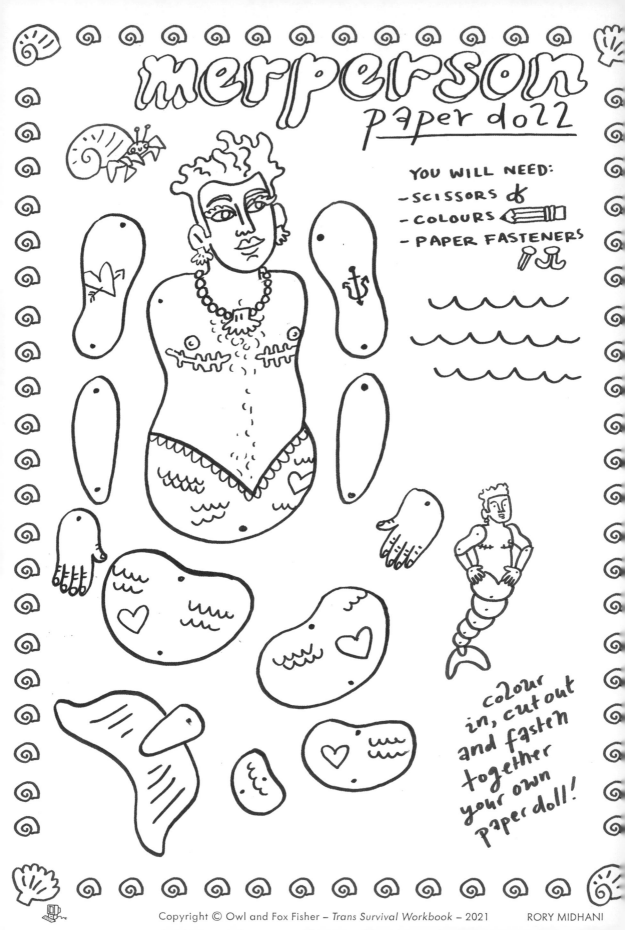

merperson
paper doll

YOU WILL NEED:
- SCISSORS
- COLOURS
- PAPER FASTENERS

colour in, cut out and fasten together your own paper doll!

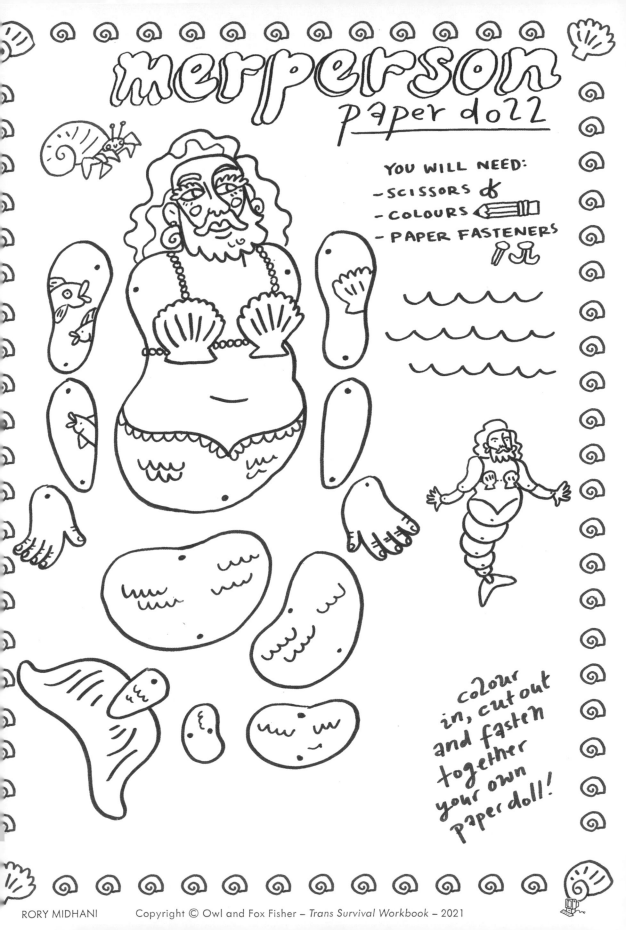

merperson
paper doll

YOU WILL NEED:
- SCISSORS
- COLOURS
- PAPER FASTENERS

colour in, cut out and fasten together your own paper doll!

IDEAL PARTNER
(IF YOU WANT ONE)

Write down the qualities you admire in your ideal partner(s). It can be things related to their personality, their traits, their style or anything you'd want in a partner. If you're happy and content being self-partnered like Emma Watson or just don't want a partner, then write down why that works best for you!

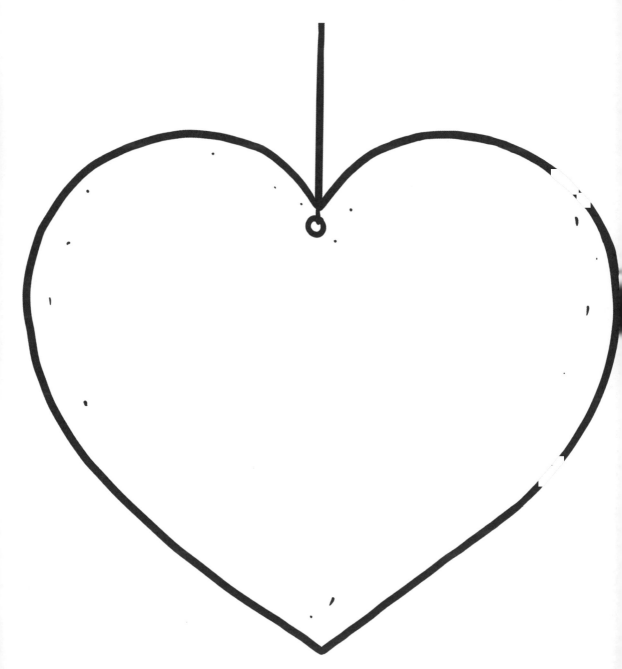

CERTIFICATE of THANKS

TO: _____

FOR BEING A **TRANS ALLY**

SIGNED _____

DATE _____

ADVICE FOR TRANS ALLIES

A question trans people get asked a lot is how cis people can be trans allies. There's no exhaustive answer or list for that, but what is some of the advice you'd give to people if they asked you? What do you need from your allies?

YOU CAN'T KNOW WHO'S TRANS OR NOT

TRANS PEOPLE EACH HAVE **DIFFERENT APPEARANCES.**

CIS PEOPLE MAY NOT HAVE THE **STEREOTYPICAL APPEARANCE** OF THEIR GENDER ASSIGNED AT BIRTH.

MANY CIS PEOPLE ENJOY **DRAG, CROSSDRESSING** OR BEING CREATIVE WITH THEIR **GENDER EXPRESSION.** THEY'RE NOT TRANS!

UNLESS THE PERSON TELLS YOU THEMSELF, IT'S **IMPOSSIBLE** TO KNOW IF THEY'RE ACTUALLY TRANS. (ALSO IT'S PROBABLY **NONE OF YOUR BUSINESS**)

RE-INVENT GENDER REVEAL PARTIES

What if gender reveal parties were something completely different than what they are now? What if they were a chance to talk about genders and stereotypes?

What if it was a party to reveal an entirely new never-before-heard-of gender identity? What if it was a party to celebrate a trans person coming out? The possibilities are endless!

Come up with your own concept for a gender reveal party and do the decorations for this room.

What if there was a spray to banish bigotry or a soap to wash away dysphoria? If only! Create your own fictional products for that quick fix:

MAKE YOUR OWN PROTEST SIGN

APPOINTMENT PREP CHECKLIST

Going in for an important appointment? Here's a checklist of a few things that can help.

- [ ] Book time off work/school
- [ ] Calculate the cost of getting there beforehand
- [ ] Chart the journey to make sure you have enough time to get there
- [ ] Bring someone with you (a friend or a relative), or at least call someone before and after
- [ ] Be on time (even early if you can)
- [ ] Prepare yourself for questions: have a think about your answers to all sorts of questions related to your gender. Just be you!
- [ ] Do something afterwards that is fun or relaxing. Appointments can be really exhausting and difficult!
- [ ] Put up boundaries. If you don't want to answer a question, you can say so and ask the person why they are asking it

Remember that the appointment is also for you to ask questions and get information. Write down the questions you have and bring them with you, so you don't forget in case you get flustered.

Anything else?

QUESTIONS TO ASK/COMMENTS

Here are a few questions you can ask during your appointment:

- What can I expect from you as my caregiver?

- If a question is uncomfortable: How is this relevant to the care you will be providing?

- How long is the wait for my next appointment?

- What is a timeline for my medical transition? How long is the wait for things like hormones, surgery, etc.?

- What sort of surgeries/treatments might be available under my care/insurance?

- Can I have counselling or can you point me towards any support groups for myself, or my family?

- Anything else?

SURGERY CHECKLIST

Going in for surgery? Here's a list of things to remember!

- Have you told everyone who needs to know?

- A fresh change of clothes

- Stuff for hygiene, e.g. toothbrush, toothpaste, shampoo, deodorant, soap, creams, hairbrush, nail clippers, tweezers

- Vitamins and pills (like oestrogen pills)

- Any after-care products you might need

- Your devices, e.g. phone, laptop, tablet, headphones

- Books

- A teddy bear, small pillow, blanket or anything that makes you feel better

- House keys

- Your wallet

- Coming home to a clean environment?

- Anything else?

Create some wording for the placards

LEWIS HANCOX

LEWIS HANCOX

ULTIMATE TRANS QUIZ

1. Who is the creator of the original transgender flag?

a) April Ashley

b) Stephen Whittle

c) Monika Helms

d) Eddie Izzard

2. Who was the first transgender person to be nominated for a prime-time Emmy?

a) Laverne Cox

b) Janet Mock

c) Logan Rozos

d) Jamie Clayton

3. In 2019, a popular youtuber and gamer raised over $160,000 for the transgender charity Mermaids by live-streaming himself playing a video game. What game was it?

a) League of Legends

b) Mario

c) Donkey Kong

d) Overwatch

4. Lilly and Lana Wachowski created a franchise that was recently con-firmed to be an allegory for being transgender. What is the name of the franchise?

a) Star Wars

b) The Matrix

c) Batman

d) Cloud Atlas

5. Who was the first openly transgender model to be on America's Next Top Model?

a) Isis King

b) Munroe Bergdorf

c) Candis Cayne

d) Geena Rocero

6. Which fictional TV series has the largest transgender cast to date?

a) *Transparent*

b) *Pose*

c) *Glee*

d) *Tales of the City*

7. What is the name of the transgender man who pioneered the use of X-rays to detect tuberculosis?

a) Alan L. Hart

b) Dr Phil

c) Billy Tipton

d) Thomas Edison

8. Which trans woman who was at the Stonewall Riots in 1969 said the following 'No Pride for some of us without liberation for all of us'?

a) Sylvia Rivera

b) Marsha P. Johnson

c) Christine Daniels

d) Susan Stryker

9. What year is it believed that the first gender reassignment surgery was performed?

a) 1974

b) 1902

c) 1930

d) 1998

10. In 1952, an American transgender woman travelled to Denmark to undergo gender reassignment surgery, and shortly afterwards became one of the first public transgender people in the world. What was her name?

a) Christine Jorgensen

b) Lili Elbe

c) Kate Bornstein

d) Felicia Elizondo

11. The famous singer Cher has a son who is trans. What is his name?

a) Chay

b) Chaz

c) Chad

e) Chiz

12. Which famous Harry Potter actor has openly spoken about their support for trans people?

a) Daniel Radcliffe

b) Rupert Grint

c) Emma Watson

d) All of the above

13. What is the name of the Olympic pole vaulter who came out in 2008?

a) Balian Buschbaum

b) Fallon Fox

c) Basil Bailyburn

d) Brian Blessed

14. Which trans woman co-wrote and co-starred in the series *Her Story*?

a) Jan Ricardo

b) Jane Pilchard

c) Jen Richards

d) Joyce Raymond

15. A British model and actress was outed as trans by the British press after she appeared in the James Bond movie *For Your Eyes Only* in 1981. What is her name?

a) Andreja Pejić

b) Caroline Cossey

c) Carmen Carrera

d) Amanda Lepore

16. What was the name of the trans character in the original *The L Word* series?

a) Max Sweeney

b) Sweeney Todd

c) Finn Howard

d) Tyler Ronan

17. What BBC series was the first UK comedy series to feature a transgender woman playing a trans character?

a) *Butterfly*

b) *Hollyoaks*

c) *Boy Meets Girl*

d) *EastEnders*

18. What was the name of the Netflix documentary that came out in 2020 about transgender people in popular film and media?

a) *The Trans List*

b) *Disclosure*

c) *The Death and Life of Marsha P. Johnson*

d) *Cisappointment*

19. What Grey's Anatomy actor came out as non-binary in 2020?

a) Sara Ramirez

b) Ellen Pompeo

c) Sandra Oh

d) Jesse Williams

20. In 2017, a trans woman became the runner-up in RuPaul's Drag Race season nine. What's her name?

a) Gia Gunn

b) Monica Beverly Hillz

c) Sonique

d) Peppermint

21. What is the term used to describe the transgender and intersex community in parts of India?

a) Calabai

b) Hijra

c) Two-spirit

d) Genderqueer

22. The transgender community in Thailand is often described by a Western term that is considered offensive. But what is the term used by the community?

a) Māhū

b) Travesti

c) Kathoey

d) Bakla

23. What word was voted as the Word of the Year 2019 by Merriam-Webster?

a) Trans

b) Non-binary

c) They

d) Gender-neutral

24. What black trans plus-size model featured in a Calvin Klein's ad campaign in 2020?

a) Jari Jones

b) Tracey Norman

c) Leyna Bloom

d) Laith Ashley

25. Travis Alabanza took the UK theatre world by storm with a performance that derived from their experience of being assaulted in public, where they had a food item thrown at them. What was the name of the piece?

a) Before I Step Outside

b) Burgerz

c) My Stubble Has No Gender

d) Tranz Talkz

Want to challenge yourself further? Advance to the more difficult stage and test your knowledge!

26. What Australian and former RuPaul's Drag Race contestant was the runner up for season six, and what major reality TV show did they win in 2018?

27. What non-binary performance artist and author wrote the book *Femme in Public* (2017)?

28. Which *Queer Eye* cast member came out as non-binary in 2019?

29. In 2020, a trans woman became the first elected mayor in France. What is her name?

30. Transgender Day of Remembrance is an annual day that is hosted all around the world. What year was it first held, and in remembrance of who?

31. What is the name of the non-binary character in the new *She-Ra* series and who is the voice actor?

32. What are the colours of the non-binary flag, and what is the correct order (top to bottom)?

33. What recent sci-fi series debuted two transgender characters in their third series in 2020, and what are the names of the actors?

34. In 2017 a non-binary actor was nominated for the Critics' Choice Television Award for their role as a non-binary character. Who is the actor and what was the series they were in?

35. What year was it first proposed by the World Health Organization that being transgender would be de-medicalized in ICD-11, and what year will that come into effect?

Answers: See 'ULTIMATE QUIZ ANSWERS' at the back of the book.

MARSHA

"PAY IT NO MIND"

JOHNSON

Graffiti your name (tag) on the wall and anything else you feel like

fox
♡
owl

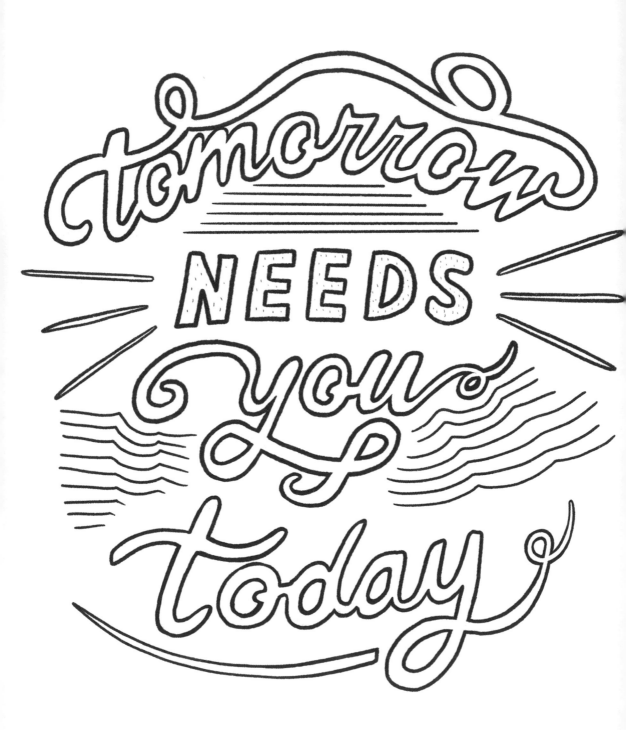

Some positive phrases

FINDING MY SUPPORT NETWORK

Whether it's family, friends or chosen family, make a list of people who support you:

FUTURE FAMILY

What do you imagine your future family to look like? Is it in a shared household with all your friends? A partner? With kids? Lots of pets? Draw your family of the future.

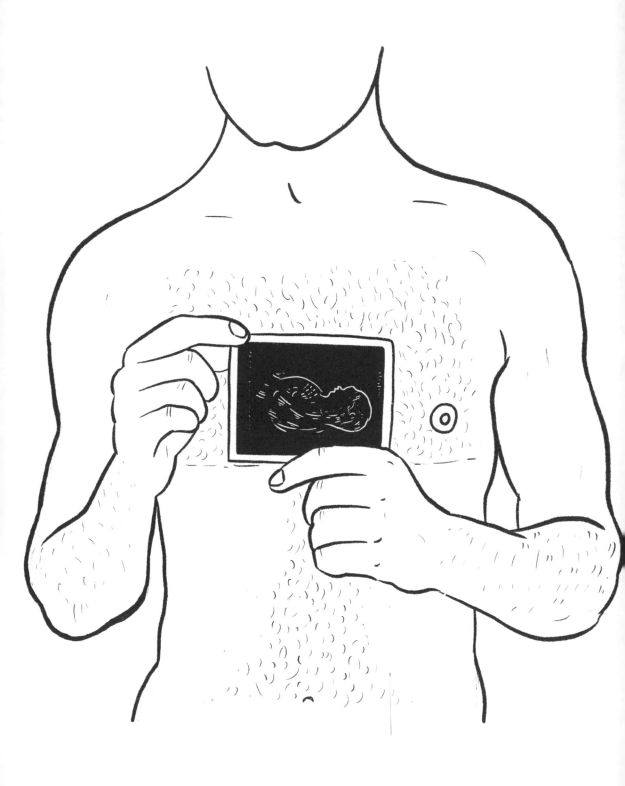

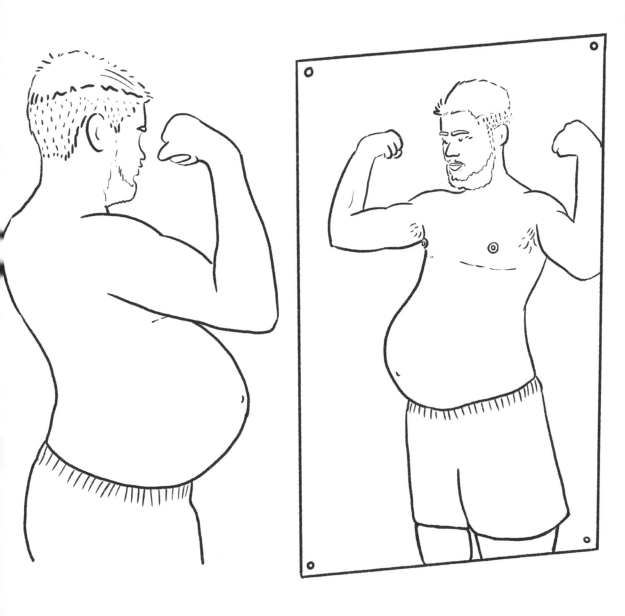

Choose Your Own Adventure

Mission:
Come out to your best friend

How to play:
Start at #1 and then make choices to see where you want to go.
Each choice has a consequence.

1.

Your best friend is having a costume party for their birthday. You have your first opportunity to really express your gender. You are planning to come out to your friend, the host at the party. You dress up as your childhood hero. Write who or what you are going as here:

What do you bring as a gift?

A birthday card
Go to 2

A home-made cake
Go to 13

2.

You arrive at the partaaay. It's already in full swing. People have really made the effort and are in full costume. You're not sure where the host is and you don't recognize anyone around. The DJ must have fallen asleep because the same song is on repeat.

What do to you do?

Go see the DJ
Go to 8

Go to the toilet
Go to 18

3.

You see your best friend off in the distance. You wave, but they don't seem to see you. By the time you get across the room, they are nowhere to be found. Your phone rings from an unknown number, but it's too loud in here to answer.

What do to you do?

Let it go to voicemail
Go to 11

Take the call in a nearby closet
Go to 16

4.

You are mid-flow when the security light comes on. Everyone can see you. You feel embarrassed and run home. Better luck next time.

5.

You hand a slice to the giraffe, who passes it down the line to others. You keep passing out slices to people until all the cake is gone. Everyone gobbles down your cake. Almost immediately someone nearby clutches their stomach. It's not long before everyone on the dance floor is feeling unwell from your cake. Awkward, you better leave the crime scene. Better luck next time. Abort mission!

6.

You get suckered in watching many recorded episodes of a strange series you've never seen before. You are intrigued by a commercial advertising a Gender Euphoria spray.

Do you buy it?

Yes
Go to 24

No
Go to 28

7.

The queue isn't as long as you think it will be. You check yourself out in the mirror. You are looking amazing!
A portal opens up in the mirror.

What do you do?

Go in the mirror
Go to 15

Leave the room
Go to 29

8.

You go to the booth, and the DJ is fast asleep! Good thing you made a party playlist last night. You sigh, move them aside and put your favourite song on. The crowd goes wild. You still can't see the host, but you do recognize one person, your childhood bully.

What do to you do?

Go talk to the bully
Go to 17

Lead a sequence dance
Go to 10

9.

You take a running leap and dive bomb into the water. What a truly special evening. You lie on your back, kicking your legs about, and you look at the stars. You see something float past and realize it's the all-important birthday card for your best friend. There was a voucher in there too. Everything is ruined.

10.

It's a first time you've worn these shoes and as you attempt a twirl, you can feel your ankle give way and come crashing down. It looks like that might need medical attention. Better luck next time.

11.

You ignore it for now and wander into a room where someone is reading fortunes.

Do you get your palm read?

Yes, of course
Go to 14

No
Go to 27

12.

You put your coat away and see a cute dog who is sleeping on the bed. You spend all evening stroking him, and don't have an opportunity to speak to anyone.

13.

You put the cake down at the snack table. Someone dressed as a giraffe cuts a slice and comments on the cake being pink, blue and white, like the trans flag. The giraffe shares that they have a cousin who is trans and pretty famous too.

Do you give them a slice?

Yes
Go to 5

No, walk away
Go to 12

14.

The fortune teller beckons for you to sit down. You offer them your hand. The fortune teller tells you you're on the right track and you're going to have a really happy and fulfilling life.

What do you do now?

Go find your friend
Go to 25

Go talk to the DJ
Go to 8

15.

That's weird. You've travelled back in time and are back at home, waiting to go out.

Got to 1

16.

It's a scammer, who tricks you into giving away all your online passwords. You spend all evening trying to block them and get to your money back. Looks like you'll never get out of the closet.

17.

You go over to where the childhood bully is dancing. The bully doesn't know who you are but compliments you on your fine DJ skills. The bully asks if you'd like a drink.

Will you accept?

No, I need the toilet
Go to 18

Yes, thanks
Go to 21

18.

Typical. There's quite a few people waiting to use the bathroom. You really want to find your friend as well.

What do you do?

Wait
Go to 7

Go look in the garden
Go to 4

19.

You try to open the door, but it's locked. You wander about aimlessly all night and fail to find your best friend. You step in doggy doo-doo and head home early. You order a giant pizza. Better luck in the future.

20.

You take a deep breath and begin speaking to them about being trans. You go into great detail about all the trials and tribulations and fears of telling them. Your best friend is nodding away at you before they have to go replenish the snack bowls. Turns out they couldn't hear any of your words over the banging music. Better luck next time.

21.

The bully runs to the bar and brings back two tall drinks with ice. The bully is full of compliments for you and your costume and asks you out. Feeling confident, you use this opportunity to tell the bully that it's you and you decline their invitation, but as you try to sassily walk away, you slip on a hotdog and fly through the air into the garden.

Go to 29

22.

They open your card and read your birthday message, which is signed off in your new name, as the real you. You best friend gives you a massive hug. Mission accomplished.

23.

You use your phone to light the way, and you call out your friend's name. You see a door that you haven't noticed before.

What do you do?

Go through the door
Go to 29

Explore more
Go to 26

24.

As if by magic, it arrives instantly. You spray it all over and feel on top of the world.

What do you do?

Go back to the party
Go to 27

Carry on watching
Go to 32

25.

You look all over the party for your best friend but you keep missing them. Someone says they've seen your friend in the basement. You open the door to the basement but it's a bit dark in there.

What do you do?

Go down the steps
Go to 23

No way
Go to 30

26.

You find an old photograph of you and your best friend from when you were much younger. You think about how far you've come since that photo was taken. You also find an old video tape.

Do you watch it?

Yes
Go to 6

No
Go to 31

27.

You bump into the host. Hurrah!

What do you do?

Give the birthday card
Go to 22

Tell them you're trans
Go to 20

28.

You go back in search of your friend, but you want to check if your outfit is still looking fierce. You need a mirror.

What do you do?

Go to the toilet
Go to 18

Go to friend's bedroom
Go to 19

29.

You discover a beautiful heated outdoor pool. You dip a toe in and it's a lovely temperature. No one is around, so you could jump in if you wanted to. You are feeling pretty confident and can't remember the last time you went swimming.

Do you take a dip?

Yes, dive in
Go to 9

Go back to party
Go to 3

30.

You get completely distracted with a party game. It brings out an extremely competitive streak in you and you spend all evening trying to win win win. What a shame you didn't get to talk with your best friend. Better luck next time you see them.

31.

You decide to go looking for your friend, but on your way up, your foot gets tangled in a wire, pulling all the electrics out, causing a massive power outage, ruining the party. Slink away.

32.

You watch all the episodes and end up falling asleep, missing the party completely. When you wake up, you realize you are going to be late for a really important appointment and have to rush out the door. Better luck next time.

TRANS PRIDE PROTEST MARCH

Create your own chants

What I'll look like when I'm older

```
V Y F  D Y S P H O R I A  A U G W Q A J S H Z  P  M
R L U Z T W Q V A S Q H D C W U X H M Y S Y  H  B
B X T T  L  U E Y  B I G E N D E R  S M Z  I  Z K  A  S
B E O D  O  R C M A R U D Q H N W J I P  D  A G L  L  T
C  V  N O  V  T Q M F S J Y U B Q E  B  I V  E  N F K  O  S
B  A  P E  E  T R A N S G E N D E R  L  D K  L  Z B  P  S
B  L  D  G  N O N B I N A R Y  V B  O  U E  T  I B  A  S
G  I  E  Y  G C X W L N F P T H C  U  I  T  E X  N  E
E  D  D  M  N A C J N Q M O V Z E  K  R  I  T  Y  G  R
N  I  G  I  B D U J S G W O V Z B  E  R  T  L  E  R  E
D  E  X  B  D  E M I G I R L  E  N  S  S  B  X  N  F  R
E  V  O  E  R  G E N D E R  V T  D  K  U  X  I  P  F  R
R  X  V  R  Y  Q U B B B R J Q G A F  E  R  E  U  X  R
F  P  Z  Q  U R C H B D K A F Y R  M  P  E  I  D  F
L  S  T  U  E X W W E E I Y D U G Z Z N  E  N  U
U  A  B  E  R  H F E T A Y R E O U K B G W A  O  I
I  F  S  R  Z F B  V A G I N O P L A S T Y  C  A  T
D  H A P P I N E S S  E W N W Y X N J T Q D Z H  R
L E I N D C  T E S T O S T E R O N E  R Z F H K  A
P U K M U X  O E S T R O G E N  A G E N D E R  A  N
W U V Y R N G Q  J O Y  D F C X P X U  R E A L  D  S
U A C P  D E A D N A M E  N X X E L H K H S K S  W
G T  P A C K E R  I L J U  M A S T E C T O M Y  I  O
Y O A N L V N V Z  T R A N S M A N  J K O S W I  N
```

Words: DYSPHORIA, BIGENDER, PHALLOPLASTY, IDENTITY, PANGENDER, TRANSGENDER, NONBINARY, LOVE, VALID, GENDERFLUID, GENDERQUEER, DEMIBOY, BLOCKERS, EXPRESSION, EUPHORIA, PUBERTY, BINDER, TUCKING, DEMIGIRL, GENDER, VAGINOPLASTY, HAPPINESS, TESTOSTERONE, OESTROGEN, AGENDER, JOY, REAL, DEADNAME, PACKER, MASTECTOMY, TRANSMAN, TRANSWOMAN

ULTIMATE QUIZ ANSWERS
(NO PEEPING!)

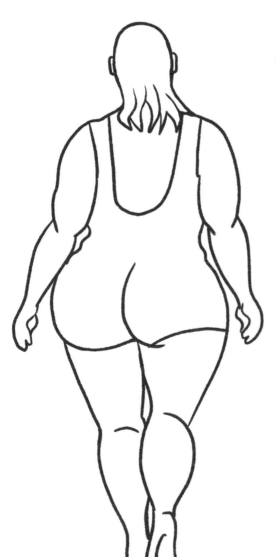

1. Monica Helms
2. Laverne Cox
3. Donkey Kong
4. The Matrix
5. Isis King
6. Pose
7. Alan L. Hart
8. Marsha P. Johnson
9. 1930
10. Christine Jorgensen
11. Chaz
12. All of the above
13. Balian Buschbaum
14. Jen Richards
15. Caroline Cossey
16. Max Sweeney
17. Boy Meets Girl
18. Disclosure
19. Sara Ramirez
20. Peppermint
21. Hijra
22. Kathoey
23. They
24. Jari Jones
25. Burgerz
26. Courtney Act/Shayne Gilberto Jenek
27. ALOK
28. Jonathan Van Ness
29. Marie Cau
30. 1999, Rita Hester
31. Double Trouble, voiced by Jacob Tobia
32. Yellow, white, purple, black
33. Star Trek: Discovery, Ian Alexander and Blu del Barrio
34. Asia Kate Dillon, Billions
35. Proposed in 2019, into effect in 2022

CHARITIES AND SUPPORT ORGANIZATIONS

UNITED KINGDOM

My Genderation
My Genderation is a film project run by Fox and Owl, celebrating trans lives and trans experiences. They have produced over 100 short films that are widely used by people seeking representation, or used as educational resources and are shown on platforms across the world.
www.mygenderation.com

Gendered Intelligence
Gendered Intelligence is a trans-led charity that specializes in supporting young trans people from ages 8–25. They aim to support and empower young transgender people and increase understanding for gender diversity in society.
http://genderedintelligence.co.uk

Mermaids
Mermaids is one of the UK's leading LGBTQ+ charities, empowering thousands of young transgender people and their families with its secure online communities, local community groups, helpline services, web resources, events and residential weekends.
https://mermaidsuk.org.uk

Stonewall UK
Stonewall UK is the UK's biggest national LGBT charity, supporting LGBT people and creating change socially, legally and within the wider community.
www.stonewall.org.uk

All About Trans
All About Trans is a project ran by the charity On Road media. The project aims to positively change how the media understands and portrays trans people. The project promotes trans voices in the media and engage media professionals and other sector professionals with trans topics in creative ways.
www.allabouttrans.org.uk

GIRES
GIRES is a UK-wide organisation whose purpose is to improve the lives of trans and gender diverse people of all ages, including those who are non-binary and non-gender.
www.gires.org.uk

Trans Actual
TransActual UK was founded by a group of British trans people in 2017 as a response to increasing press hostility, transphobia and misinformation.
www.transactual.org.uk

QTIPOC Narratives
Brighton based QTIBPoC collective, creating workshops, art, zines and alternative mental health space.
Twitter: @qtipocnarrative
Facebook: QTIPoC Narrative

LGBT Switchboard
A UK National Helpline for LGBTQ people.
https://switchboard.lgbt

UNITED STATES OF AMERICA

GLAAD
GLAAD is the leading source for fair representation of the LGBTQIA+ community in the media. From coverage of significant events to accurate depictions of queer stories in film and television, GLAAD is there to enforce visibility and accountability.
www.glaad.org

The Human Rights Campaign
SnAPco
SNaPCo builds power of Black trans and queer people to force systemic divestment from the prison industrial complex and invest in community support.
www.snap4freedom.org

GLSEN
GLSEN was founded in 1990 by a group of teachers in Massachusetts who wanted to improve the bullying and discrimination problem against LGBTQ students in schools from grades K-12.
www.glsen.org

Black Aids Institution
Founded in 1999, the Black Aids Institution (BAI) works to end the Black HIV epidemic through policy, advocacy, and high-quality direct HIV services.
https://blackaids.org

National Centre for Transgender Equality
The National Center for Transgender Equality was founded in 2003 and has since made it their mission to advocate and push for policy change that protects the freedom and liberties of transgender Americans.
https://transequality.org

The Trans Cultural District
Founded by three Black trans women in 2017, the Transgender District is the first legally recognized transgender district in the world. Encompassing six blocks in San Francisco, this collective works to economically empower the trans community while educating and celebrating the legacy of the transgender movement.
www.transgenderdistrictsf.com

The Trevor Project
The Trevor Project is a national crisis and suicide prevention hotline for LGBTQ teens and young adults in the US.
www.thetrevorproject.org

Immigration Equality
Immigration Equality is an immigrant rights organization helping LGBTQ and HIV positive immigrants in the United States and around the world find safety and fair treatment.
https://immigrationequality.org

YOUTUBERS

Alex Bertie
A trans guy making transgender content and vlogs about his life.
www.youtube.com/c/TheRealAlexBertie

Angelina and Niko, Days of our Wives
A cis and a trans woman who are married, sharing content about their lives together.
www.youtube.com/c/DaysofOurWives

Cat Blaque
A trans woman of colour who does opinion essays, is an illustrator and self-proclaimed thrift store addict.
www.youtube.com/c/KatBlaque

Chandler Wilson
An agender person creating videos about LGBTQ identities and their personal life.
www.youtube.com/c/ChandlerNWilson

Chase Ross
A trans guy who vlogs about his personal life and transgender issues in general.
www.youtube.com/c/uppercaseCHASE1

Contrapoints (Natalie Wynn)
An American video essayist that explores politics, gender, ethics, race and philosophy.
www.youtube.com/c/ContraPoints

Curio
A non-binary content creator that does videos on popular culture like video games, films or series.
www.youtube.com/c/CurioVids

Gigi Gorgeous
A trans woman who is a long term creator on YouTube, creating anything from vlogs, to beauty tutorials, to writing books.
www.youtube.com/c/GigiGorgeous

Jake Edwards
A non-binary musician that creates music and vlogs about their life.
www.youtube.com/c/JakeFTMagic

Jammidodger (Jamie)
A trans guy who does vlogs and videos on trans issues, popular topics, relationships or anything in between.
www.youtube.com/c/Jammidodger94

Jeffrey Marsh
A genderfluid activist, creating content about rams issues and their personal life.
www.youtube.com/c/JeffreyMarsh77

Jess (Jackdaw) Burns
An all-round creative, sharing art, animation and TTRPG supplements.
www.youtube.com/channel/UC3HyvfrwscLKtE_NmO QfWGw

Katy Montgomerie
A feminist and LGBT advocate who creates content about her life, gender and music.
www.youtube.com/c/KatyMontgomerie

Mila Jam
A trans woman of colour, who creates music covers and original music.
www.youtube.com/user/milajammusic

Miles Jay
A non-binary trans femme person of colour who does sketches, parodies and beauty tutorials.
www.youtube.com/c/MilesJaiProductions

Nikkie Tutorials
A trans woman from the Netherlands who does beauty tutorial videos.
www.youtube.com/c/nikkietutorials

Noah Finnce
A trans guy who is a musician and popular vlogger.
www.youtube.com/c/NoahFinnce

Princess Joules
A Canadian trans woman of colour who creates content about her personal life, make up and fashion.
www.youtube.com/user/princessjoules

Riley J. Dennis
A lesbian who happens to be a trans woman, who makes videos about trans issues, and video essays about various TV shows.
www.youtube.com/rileyjaydennis

Ryan Jacob Flores
A trans man of colour sharing vlogs about his life and transgender issues.
www.youtube.com/c/RyanJacobsFlores

Sam Collins
A trans guy who creates video content about LGBT issues, gender and popular culture.
www.youtube.com/user/SupraMan38

Shonalika
A non-binary person of colour who is a musical video essayist that does videos on transgender issues.
www.youtube.com/c/Shonalika

Stef Sanjati
A trans woman who is very open about having Waardenburg syndrome, who creates content on trans issues, beauty tutorials and now streams video games on twitch.
www.twitch.tv/thestefsanjati

Trinity, Beauty with Trinity
A trans woman of colour who makes beauty tutorials and vlogs about her life.
www.youtube.com/user/BeautyWithTrinity

Ts Madison
A trans woman of colour who does sketches, parodies and videos about her life.
www.youtube.com/c/TsMadisonHinton

TRANS TEEN SURVIVAL GUIDE
Owl Fisher and Fox Fisher

£12.99/$17.95 | ISBN: 978 1 78592 341 8
eISBN: 978 1 78450 662 9

Frank, friendly and funny, this must-read guide is packed full of advice from authors who understand the realities and complexities of growing up trans. Readers will come away empowered and armed with practical advice on how to navigate everything from coming out, clothes and pronouns, to wearing binders or packers, hormone therapy and self-care.

THE TRANS SELF-CARE WORKBOOK
A Coloring Book and Journal for Trans and Non-Binary People
Theo Lorenz

£14.99/$19.95 | ISBN: 978 1 78775 343 3
eISBN: 978 1 78775 344 0

Radical and emotionally raw, this book pushes the boundaries of trans representation by redefining 'trans' as an identity with its own power and strength, that goes beyond the gender binary. Features intimate conversations with leading figures in the trans community, such as Kate Bornstein, Travis Alabanza, Josephine Jones and Glamrou.

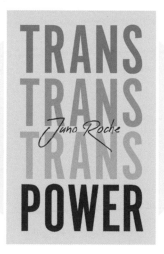

TRANS POWER
Own Your Gender
Juno Roche

£12.99/$18.95 | ISBN: 978 1 78775 019 7
eISBN: 978 1 78775 020 3

A creative workbook for the trans and non-binary community, including colouring pages, journaling prompts and reflective exercises. Drawing on CBT and mindfulness techniques, topics include euphoria and dysphoria, coming out and building relationships, promoting the message that although no experience is identical to another, nobody is alone.